THE NEZ PERCE

A First Americans Book

Virginia Driving Hawk Sneve

illustrated by Ronald Himler

Holiday House/New York

ACKNOWLEDGMENTS

The quotations of Old Joseph, Toohulhulsote, Wounded Head, and Chief Joseph are from *I Have Spoken: American History Through the Voices of the Indians*, by Virginia Irving Armstrong, ed. (Athens, OH: Swallow Press/Ohio University Press, 1971).

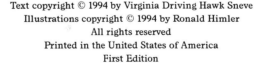

Library of Congress Cataloging-in-Publication Data
Sneve, Virginia Driving Hawk.
The Nez Perce / Virginia Driving Hawk Sneve ; illustrated by
Ronald Himler. — 1st ed.
p.   cm. — (A First Americans book)
Includes index.
ISBN 0-8234-1090-0
1. Nez Percé Indians — History — Juvenile literature.   2. Nez Percé
Indians — Social life and customs — Juvenile literature.   [1. Nez
Percé Indians.   2. Indians of North America.]   I. Himler, Ronald,
ill.   II. Title.   III. Series: Sneve, Virginia Driving Hawk.   First
Americans book.
E99.N5S64   1994   93-38598   CIP   AC
973'.04974 — dc20

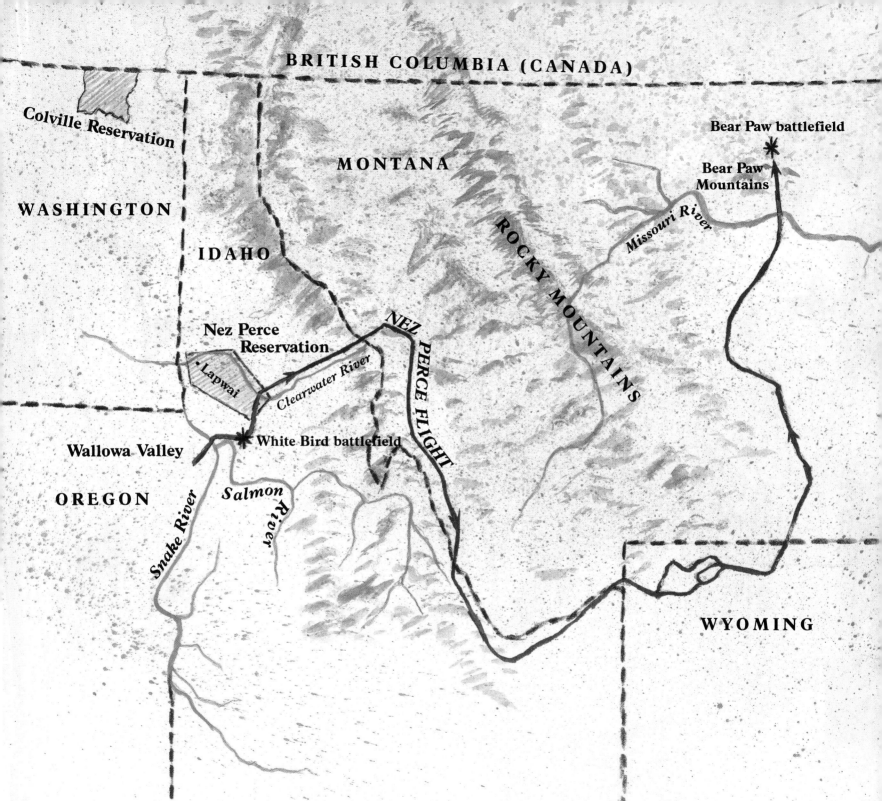

BRITISH COLUMBIA (CANADA)

Colville Reservation

WASHINGTON

MONTANA

IDAHO

ROCKY MOUNTAINS

Bear Paw battlefield

Bear Paw
Mountains

Missouri River

Nez Perce
Reservation

·Lapwai

Clearwater River

NEZ PERCE FLIGHT

Wallowa Valley

White Bird battlefield

OREGON

Salmon River

Snake River

WYOMING

CREATION

This country holds your father's body.
OLD JOSEPH

Long ago there was a greedy monster who ate everything in its path. Coyote decided that he must rescue all that the monster had devoured. He thought hard and finally had a plan. Coyote hid a sharp bone in his mouth. Then he tied one end of a grapevine around a rock and the other end around his waist so that if he were eaten he could pull himself out of the monster's stomach.

The monster came and swallowed Coyote, breaking the vine. He also devoured plants, trees, water, and other animals. Once inside the monster, Coyote took the sharp bone from his mouth and stabbed the creature in the heart. The monster cried out and died. Coyote escaped through the dead monster's open mouth. As Coyote emerged so did all of the other things the monster had swallowed.

The dead monster was as large as a mountain, and Coyote wondered what to do with it. Fox suggested, "Why don't you cut the monster up and make something good out of the pieces?"

Coyote asked the Great Spirit for help. Then he cut up the monster and threw the pieces far out over the mountains. Wherever a bit of the monster landed, the Great Spirit created a new tribe of humans. After all of the monster was scattered, there were no people in the place where Fox and Coyote stood. Only drops of blood were left from the monster. Coyote again prayed for help, and the Great Spirit caused the drops of blood to become humans who called themselves the "Chopunnish," or "Nimipu," both names meaning "the real people."

A NEW NAME

A few more years and the white men will be all around you.
OLD JOSEPH

Some scholars believe that in the 1600s French-Canadian fur trappers were the first white men to meet the Chopunnish. The trappers called them *Nez Percé*, "pierced nose," because some of the Indians wore a bone or shell ornament that they had pierced through the space between their nostrils. Years later American trappers used the same name, and pronounced it "nez purse."

Other scholars say that the name was given to the Chopunnish by William Clark. Co-leader of the Lewis and Clark Expedition, he traveled through Nez Perce territory while exploring the West in 1805.

HOMELAND

The earth is part of my body, and I never gave up the earth.
TOOHULHULSOTE

The Nez Perce whom the white men met lived in the tall mountains between the Cascades and the Rockies in what are now the states of Washington, Oregon, Idaho, and Montana. The tribe was made up of about seventy small, independent bands whose villages were several miles apart. Because the villages weren't crowded together, there were enough hunting and fishing grounds to meet the Indians' needs.

A village had several houses clustered along a stream. Some were round and built on top of large holes dug four feet into the ground. Their walls and roofs were covered with woven reed mats. Others were longhouses shaped like an A, with the lower part dug into the ground and the upper covered with reed mats.

Twenty families often lived in a longhouse. Each family cooked over a separate fire in a trench that ran down the middle of the inside. There was a smoke hole in the center of the roof. There were several openings on the sides of the house. These were used for going in and out, to provide air for the fires, and to ventilate the house.

sweat hut

Near the stream, each lodge had a sweat hut that was used for daily baths. Hot stones were carried into the hut, where people sat and sweated. Afterward, they plunged into the cold stream to wash away dirt, germs, and perspiration. Sometimes a medicine man held a cleansing ceremony in the hut to purify the spirit before a special event, or to cure sickness.

In the summers when the Nez Perce left their houses to gather food, they took the mats from the walls and roofs. The wind and rain came through the open lodges and cleaned them while the people were away. During the summer, the Nez Perce lived in small tepees covered with the woven mats from the roofs and walls of their winter homes.

FOOD GATHERING

So long as the earth keeps me, I want to be left alone.
TOOHULHULSOTE

camas plant

camas bulb

The women and girls picked wild berries. In the early spring, the Nez Perce used a sharp, crutch-handled stick to dig up the bulblike roots of the kouse plant. The bulbs were eaten raw and tasted like turnips.

The women and girls also dug up camas bulbs. Camas is a wild lily with blue flowers on a tall, single stalk. Its root, an onion-shaped bulb, is juicy, sweet, and crunchy. The workers used a stone pestle and wooden mortar to grind the camas roots for making mush or cakes.

During early summer, when the camas bulbs were ripe, the Nez Perce bands met to gather the bulbs, see old friends and relatives, play games, dance, and trade. They wore their best clothes for this important festival, which no one missed.

Besides gathering food, the women made pottery. They also wove coiled, watertight baskets in which they heated water with hot stones. They used the baskets to boil roots and meat. They sometimes cooked meat, too, by skewering it on sticks stuck in the ground around an open fire.

The men made bowls, spoons, and cups from wood and the horns of mountain sheep.

In the late spring and early summer, the whole village went to the rivers to get salmon. The men used hooks and line, spears, harpoons, dip nets, traps, and weirs to catch the fish. Traps and weirs were made by the men of several villages who divided the catch. The traps were a kind of cage into which the fish swam and couldn't get out. The men scooped the trapped fish out of the water. Weirs were temporary barricades which dammed the water. This made the fish easier to catch. The women split, cleaned, and dried the salmon on racks over smoky pits. The dried, smoked salmon, as well as the dried camas bulbs, were stored in baskets during the long winters.

MEN

Let me be a free man . . .
CHIEF JOSEPH (OLD JOSEPH'S SON)

horn bow

Each village had three or four elderly men who formed a council. It was headed informally by one highly respected man or chief. The elders met to discuss village concerns. There were no laws to enforce, but the chief persuaded others to do what was necessary for the good of the village. The people respected each other's opinions, but if one person did not agree with the headman or council, he could join another village.

The Nez Perce hunted deer, elk, moose, bear, and antelope to eat. The elderly men made bows from yew, ash, or willow, but the most prized were made from the big horn sheep's large, curved horns. A horn bow was more flexible than a wooden one and could shoot arrows farther. The Nez Perce made the horn bow even after they acquired guns from white men.

13

Nez Perce men were not only skilled at hunting, they were also fearless in combat. A warrior planted a special staff on the battlefield and there he fought. He would not move from that spot until he was relieved by another or the battle ended.

The Nez Perce's main enemies were the Bannock, but they sometimes had battles with the Blackfeet and Cheyenne as well. The Nez Perce fought mainly to protect their hunting lands and families.

In times of war, any brave young man could take charge, and others followed him if they believed he was the right one to lead.

CHILDREN AND FAMILY LIFE

baby in cradleboard

This country holds your father's body.
Never sell the bones of your father and your mother.
OLD JOSEPH

Nez Perce families often had many children. When a child was born, relatives gave gifts and held feasts to honor the newborn.

Babies were placed in cradleboards on the mother's back. Sometimes the mother removed the cradleboard and set it where she could watch the baby as she did her chores.

A boy practiced hunting and fishing with his grandfather. A girl learned household chores from her grandmother. Grandparents told stories that not only entertained the children, but taught them tribal history and proper behavior as well. Uncles, aunts, cousins, and older brothers and sisters helped care for and train the children.

At about age three, girls and boys began to help with family tasks. They went along on hunts, fishing trips, and on journeys to dig roots. Boys had toy bows and girls had small digging sticks. By the age of six, children were important helpers in gathering food.

When a boy in his early teens had his first successful hunt or fish catch, a ceremony was held and the meat or fish was served to adult males. The Nez Perce believed that if a well-known hunter or fisherman ate the boy's first game or catch, the boy would become a good provider. A similar ceremony was held for girls. Women known for their skill in food gathering would eat the roots and berries that a girl picked or dug up for the first time all by herself.

SPIRIT HELPERS

We may quarrel with men sometimes about things on earth,
but we never quarrel about the Great Spirit.

CHIEF JOSEPH

The Nez Perce believed the Great Spirit was the father of all things and that the earth was the mother. Therefore, the Nez Perce were related to all of nature. Animals and birds had special powers, and humans had to seek a spirit helper. This spirit aided and guided an individual all through life.

Between the ages of ten and thirteen, Nez Perce boys and girls were expected to seek a vision in which their spirit helper would appear. If they had no vision, they believed they would have meaningless lives. Many sought visions several times before receiving one.

A medicine man interpreted the visions and was in charge of all ceremonies. He also treated the ill and performed special rituals to help the hunters find game.

THE COMING OF THE HORSE

This animal hemene *once gave me by its spirit the strength and power . . .*
WOUNDED HEAD

In 1805 William Clark and other white men of the Lewis and Clark Expedition met the Nez Perce near the Clearwater River while exploring territory between the Missouri River and the West Coast. They found the Nez Perce to be skilled horsemen with large herds of horses.

Sometime between 1700 and 1730, the Nez Perce are believed to have traded goods for horses from the Shoshone, a neighboring tribe in the mountains. The Nez Perce homeland was ideal for raising horses, since it provided rich summer grazing, plenty of water, and winter shelter in the deep mountain valleys. The mountains helped prevent the animals from leaving the valley and kept horse thieves out.

Once the Nez Perce had horses, they no longer needed to walk to the camas gathering or to the salmon runs. The horses made it easier to hunt in the mountains, and because of better hunting the Nez Perce had more meat to eat.

CLOTHING

Good words will not get my people a home
where they can live in peace and take care of themselves.
CHIEF JOSEPH

woven hat

woman's leggings

With horses, the Nez Perce were able to travel farther east into the plains to hunt buffalo. From the animal's skin, they made robes to wear in the winter. The men wore their hair in a high pouf above their foreheads, with the rest in long braids. They began to wear the war bonnet of the Plains Indians and fringed buckskin shirts, leggings, and moccasins.

Nez Perce women and girls started to put on fringed buckskin clothing, decorated with elk teeth, quillwork, and beads. The women wore a woven round hat adorned with quills and tassels. Their moccasins were knee-high and trimmed with quillwork or beads.

THE BOSTONS

I have heard talk and talk . . .
Good words do not last long unless they amount to something.
CHIEF JOSEPH

William Clark

Henry Spaulding

The Nez Perce were friendly and helpful to the white men who visited them. They showed the fur trappers and traders the way through the mountains. They drew maps of the Columbia River that helped Lewis and Clark reach the Pacific Ocean. The Nez Perce considered William Clark to be their personal friend.

The Nez Perce were interested in the way the white men could talk to each other on paper. They wanted to learn to read and write. In 1831 a Nez Perce delegation went to St. Louis to see their friend, William Clark, who was now U.S. Commissioner of Indian Affairs. The delegation asked him to set up schools for Indian children. They did not realize that the white missionaries who taught in the schools would insist that the Nez Perce become Christians if they wanted to be educated.

Because the missionaries came from the East, the Nez Perce called them and other white people "Bostons."

The Nez Perce's first teacher was Eliza Spaulding. Her husband, Henry Spaulding, preached to the Indians. At first the Indians listened to Mr. Spaulding, but then they came to resent him because he whipped the Indians who would not become Christians. Mr. Spaulding also made them farm the land around the mission. The Nez Perce believed it was wrong to dig up Mother Earth, but if they wanted their children to attend school, the parents had to become Christian farmers.

In 1840 former fur trappers opened the Oregon Trail for white settlers to travel to the Northwest. The settlers brought diseases with them. In 1846 hundreds of Nez Perce died in a smallpox epidemic. The next year measles killed hundreds more.

In 1853, the U.S. government created Washington Territory. It included Nez Perce land. Isaac Stevens, the territory's first governor, wanted to open the area to white settlement, and he began treaty negotiations with the tribes. In 1855, the Treaty of Walla created reservations for the Yakima, Umatilla, and Nez Perce tribes. The Indians did not want the treaty, but they signed it because they knew there would be war if they did not. Stevens told the Indians that they would not have to move to the reservations until the U.S. Senate and president approved the treaty. He also promised not to let settlers into the region until the treaty became law.

THE RESERVATION

You white people get together and measure the earth and then divide it . . .
                                                    TOOHULHULSOTE

**Hallalhotsoot
(Lawyer)**

Gold was discovered in Oregon in 1850 and hundreds of white prospectors crossed through Nez Perce land on their way to get rich. More gold was found in the Clearwater River on Nez Perce land. At first the U.S. government tried to keep the miners out, but white men ignored the government and the treaty.

White settlers and miners urged the government to redraw the boundaries so that the gold sites would lie outside of the Nez Perce reservation. The new area became known as the Lapwai Reservation. In May 1863 a treaty council was held, and the Nez Perce became a divided people. One group accepted a new treaty that promised them money, schools, houses, and plowed land. A second group was

23

against the treaty because the new, smaller reservation did not include the
Wallowa Valley which was their favorite place. A third and smaller group
believed it would be best to kill or drive the white men from their land. The
government wanted only one leader for all of the Nez Perce, but the three groups
decided to act as they had in the past; each band with its own chief would make a
separate treaty.

Old Joseph leading his people into the Wallowa Valley

The U.S. government did not like this decision and had Chief Hallalhotsoot of the first group sign the treaty for all of the Nez Perce. The white men called Hallalhotsoot "Lawyer" because of his skill in presenting arguments.

Old Joseph was the chief of the second group who refused to give up land. He would not live on the reservation and led his people into the Wallowa Valley, where he died and was buried in 1871. His son, Young Joseph, became chief, and like his father, he wanted only to be left alone to live in the beautiful valley.

WAR

I remembered all the insults I had endured and my blood was on fire.
Chief Joseph

Chief Joseph

Joseph and other Nez Perce who would not live on the reservation were called "nontreaty Indians." In 1877 the government insisted that all of the Nez Perce move onto the reservation, and that they had thirty days to do so.

Joseph and the other chiefs finally agreed to move because they did not want a war that would destroy their people. The Nez Perce sadly began the trek to the reservation.

Wahlitits, a young man whose father had been killed by a white man, decided that he had to avenge his father's death. He and two other young warriors raided white settlements along the Salmon River, killing three men and wounding

another. When the Nez Perce heard of the killings, some of the younger men formed a war party against the whites.

Word of the killings reached Joseph and the other chiefs. They did not want war, again because they worried that many Nez Perce would be killed by the U.S. Army. The chiefs still hoped to negotiate peace, so they moved to White Bird Canyon to meet with the soldiers. But the troopers began shooting before there was a chance to speak of peace.

The Nez Perce defended themselves and drove the soldiers out of the canyon. Joseph then led about eight-hundred Nez Perce toward Canada where he hoped they would be safe.

The U.S. government still wanted the Nez Perce to go to the reservation. The army, led by General Oliver Otis Howard, chased the Nez Perce across the mountains, through Yellowstone National Park, and over the Missouri River. The Indians traveled as fast as they could on the terrible journey of more than a thousand miles. The Nez Perce were exhausted, hungry, and sick. Many of them were wounded in encounters with the pursuing army.

They stopped to rest in the Bear Paw Mountains in Montana, only thirty miles from Canada. There Colonel Nelson Miles's troops attacked them. Finally, after a five-day battle, Chief Joseph and his weary Nez Perce surrendered.

CHIEF JOSEPH'S SURRENDER

I am tired of fighting.
CHIEF JOSEPH

Joseph asked to return to Idaho, but he was taken to North Dakota and from there he and his band were sent to a Kansas reservation. Many Nez Perce died in Kansas because they were unused to the heat and humidity of the plains. In about 1881, 200 of the Kansan Nez Perce were allowed to return to the Lapwai Reservation in Idaho. But Joseph and about 150 others were sent to the Colville Reservation in Washington where Joseph died in 1904.

TODAY

It makes my heart sick when I remember
all the good words that are broken promises . . .
CHIEF JOSEPH

The Nez Perce still live on the Lapwai Reservation in Idaho. In 1990, the U.S. census counted 4,113 Nez Perce in the United States. About 3,000 of that group lived on the Idaho reservation. Today many work at farming or lumbering, but others have gone to college and are doctors, lawyers, teachers, nurses, and engineers. Some members of the Nez Perce have scattered as if Coyote had thrown pieces of the monster all over the world.

Chief Joseph was an eloquent orator in his native language, but even when translated into English, his words had power. His last speech, given when he surrendered at Bear Paw, caused many white soldiers to weep.

"Our chiefs are killed. Looking Glass is dead. Toohulhulsote is dead. The old men are all dead. It is the young men who say yes and no. He who led the young men is dead.

"It is cold and we have no blankets. The little children are freezing to death.

"My people, some of them, have run away to the hills and have no blankets, no food; no one knows where they are — perhaps freezing to death.

"I want time to look for my children and see how many I can find. Maybe I shall find them among the dead.

"Hear me, my chiefs. I am tired; my heart is sick and sad.

"From where the sun now stands I will fight no more forever."

INDEX